CHILI & HAMBURGER

Copyright © 1995 The Triangle Group, Ltd.
All Rights Reserved. No part of this book may be reproduced or copied in any format
without written permission from the publisher. Popular Brands Cookbooks™ is a trademark of
MODERN PUBLISHING
A Division of Unisystems, Inc. / New York, New York 10022
Printed in the U.S.A.

Note: Although the recipes contained in this book have been tested by the manufacturers and have been carefully edited by the publisher, the publisher and the manufacturers cannot be held responsible for any ill effects caused by errors in the recipes, or by spoiled ingredients, unsanitary conditions, incorrect preparation procedures or any other cause beyond their control.

GINGERED TURKEY BURGERS

vegetable cooking spray
2 lbs (910 g) NORBEST
    Ground Turkey
2 tbs (30 ml) minced ginger
2 tsp (10 ml) minced garlic
1 tsp (5 ml) sage
1 tsp (5 ml) thyme
1 tsp (5 ml) salt
½ tsp (3 ml) pepper
8 hamburger buns, toasted
Chinese hot mustard

Spray cold grill rack with vegetable cooking spray. Preheat charcoal grill for direct-heat cooking.

In medium bowl, combine turkey, ginger, sage, thyme, salt and pepper. Evenly divide turkey mixture into 8 burgers, approximately 3½ inches in diameter. Grill turkey burgers 5-6 minutes per side or until 160°F (71°C) is reached on meat thermometer and meat is no longer pink in center. To serve, spread bottom half of each bun with Chinese mustard. Place burger on bun and top with other half of buns. Serves 8.

Approximate nutritional analysis per serving: Calories 321, Protein 24 g, Carbohydrates 23 g, Fat 14 g, Cholesterol 57 mg, Sodium 584 mg

Opposite: Camp Tacos

OLIVE-TURKEY TAMALE BAKE

4 ears corn, with husks
1 lb (455 g) ground turkey
2 tbs (30 ml) vegetable oil
1 cup (240 ml) CALIFORNIA
    ripe olive wedges
½ cup (120 ml) chopped green
    onion, half green, half bulbs
1 tbs (15 ml) chili powder
1½ cups (355 ml) grated pepper
jack or Monterey Jack cheese

Husk corn, tearing husk as little as possible. Save outer husks, cleaning off the silk. Drop the corn and saved husks into large pot of boiling water. Return to boil and simmer 5 minutes. Drain through colander. Meanwhile, sauté turkey in oil in skillet over high heat until browned. Using large knife, quickly slice corn kernels from cobs and add olives, onion and chili powder to turkey. Sauté 2 minutes longer. Remove from heat and stir in cheese. Line bottom 1½-qt casserole with half the softened husks. Turn turkey filling over husks and make a layer of remaining husks on top, tucking in at edges. Cover and bake at 425°F (220°C) for 20 minutes or until hot in center. Serves 4.

Approximate nutritional analysis per serving: Calories 540, Protein 40 g, Carbohydrates 11 g, Fat 38 g, Cholesterol 116 mg, Sodium 511 mg

CAMP TACOS

8 taco shells
1 lb (455 g) ground turkey
    or lean ground beef
1 - 15 oz can (450 g) pinto beans,
    drained
4 oz (120 g) "mild Mexican"
    pasteurized
    process cheese spread*
½ cup (120 ml) chopped
    CALIFORNIA ripe olives
shredded lettuce
chopped tomato
extra chopped olives for topping

* The cheese spread is usually found on grocery shelf, not under refrigeration.

To warm taco shells, place them on metal camp plate, cover with foil and set plate on top of pot of water that has been brought to a boil then removed from heat, or warm in oven. Sauté ground turkey in well-oiled skillet over high heat until cooked. Stir in pinto beans, the cheese spread and chopped olives. Heat, stirring until hot through. To serve, spoon turkey mixture into taco shells. Add lettuce, tomato and extra olives to shells. Serves 4.

Approximate nutritional analysis per serving: Calories 604, Protein 43 g, Carbohydrates 40 g, Fat 32 g, Cholesterol 105 mg, Sodium 1152 mg

LAMB PASTITSIO

- 1½ cups (355 ml) uncooked elbow macaroni
- 5 tbs (75 ml) butter or margarine, divided
- ⅓ cup (80 ml) all-purpose flour
- 3 cups (720 ml) milk
- ½ cup (120 ml) grated kefalotiri or Parmesan cheese
- 1 tbs (15 ml) olive oil
- 1 lb (455 g) ground lamb
- ½ cup (120 ml) finely chopped onion
- 2 cloves garlic, crushed
- ½ tsp (3 ml) dried oregano leaves, crushed
- ¼ tsp (1 ml) salt
- ¼ tsp (1 ml) ground cinnamon
- ⅛ tsp (.5 ml) freshly ground black pepper
- dash ground nutmeg
- 1 - 10 oz can (300 g) peeled whole tomatoes, undrained
- ¼ cup (60 ml) tomato paste
- 4 eggs, divided
- ⅓ cup (80 ml) soft bread crumbs

Prepare macaroni according to package directions; drain. Rinse with cold water; drain. Meanwhile melt 4 tbs butter in heavy saucepan; stir in flour. Gradually stir in milk; cook until thickened, stirring occasionally. Add cheese; stir until melted. Cover; cool slightly. Heat oil in large skillet; brown ground lamb, onion and garlic; stirring occasionally to break up lamb. Pour off drippings. Sprinkle oregano, salt, cinnamon, pepper and nutmeg over lamb. Drain liquid from tomatoes into small bowl; break up and reserve tomatoes. Combine tomato liquid and tomato paste; stir into lamb mixture. Cook over medium heat 5 minutes; stir in tomatoes. Separate 1 egg; combine yolk and 1 cup white sauce in large bowl; reserve. Beat together egg white, remaining 3 eggs and remaining white sauce in large bowl; gently stir in macaroni. Place half of the macaroni mixture in bottom of buttered 8x8-inch baking dish. Spoon lamb mixture evenly over macaroni; spoon remaining macaroni mixture over lamb. Pour reserved egg yolk mixture over macaroni. Melt remaining 1 tbs butter; stir in bread crumbs. Sprinkle over macaroni mixture. Bake in moderate, 375°F (190°C), oven 45 minutes. Reduce heat to moderate, 325°F (165°C); continue baking 15 minutes. Let stand 15 minutes before serving. Serves 6.

Approximate nutritional analysis per serving:
Calories 543, Protein 32 g,
Carbohydrates 40 g, Fat 28 g,
Cholesterol 288 mg, Sodium 618 mg

Lamb Pastitsio
(Courtesy National Livestock and Meat Board)

TURKEY BARBECUE MEATLOAF

1 lb (455 g) NORBEST
   Ground Turkey
1 cup (240 ml) chopped onion
½ cup (120 ml) seasoned
   bread crumbs
½ cup (120 ml) grated carrots
½ cup (120 ml) bottled barbecue
   sauce, divided
2 tsp (10 ml) Worcestershire
   sauce
1 tsp (5 ml) minced garlic
¾ tsp (4 ml) pepper
vegetable cooking spray

In medium bowl combine turkey,
onion, bread crumbs, carrots, ¼ cup
barbecue sauce, Worcestershire, garlic
and pepper. In 9-inch pie plate,
sprayed with vegetable cooking spray,
shape meat mixture into round loaf.
Drizzle top of loaf with remaining
barbecue sauce. Bake at 350°F (180°C)
35-40 minutes or until meat thermometer reaches 160°F (71°C) when
inserted in center of meat loaf, juices
run clear and meat is no longer pink.
Serves 6.

Approximate nutritional analysis per serving:
Calories 178, Protein 16 g,
Carbohydrates 14 g, Fat 7 g,
Cholesterol 55 mg, Sodium 528 mg

QUARTERBACK MEATLOAF

1 egg or egg substitute
1 lb (455 g) lean ground beef *or*
   ½ lb (230 g) *each* ground beef
   and pork
1 tsp (5 ml) salt
1 tsp (5 ml) IMPERIAL
   Granulated Sugar
⅛ tsp (.5 ml) pepper
1 tsp (5 ml) lemon juice
¼ cup (60 ml) chopped onion
½ cup (120 ml) bread crumbs
½ cup (120 ml) pork and beans
12 strips pimiento
¼ cup (60 ml) ketchup

Set oven at 400°F (205°C). Beat egg in
mixing bowl. Add all ingredients except
pimiento and ketchup. Mix lightly with
fork. Shape into four loaves shaped like
footballs. Place loaves on baking sheet
and brush with catsup mixed with 1 tbs
water. Bake 25 minutes. Lift with large
spoon onto serving dish. Put strips of
pimiento on top of each loaf in X
design. Serves 4.

Approximate nutritional analysis per serving:
Calories 396, Protein 33 g,
Carbohydrates 20 g, Fat 20 g,
Cholesterol 156 mg, Sodium 1017 mg

Turkey Barbecue Meatloaf

STUFFED CABBAGE

1 large head cabbage
1 can tomatoes
2 chopped onions
1 lb (455 g) EMPIRE KOSHER
    Ground Turkey
    or Ground Chicken
2 chicken bouillon cubes
1 grated onion
1 tsp (5 ml) salt
½ cup (120 ml) rice, partially
    cooked and drained
1 beaten egg
4 tbs (60 ml) lemon juice
3 tbs (45 ml) brown sugar

Pour boiling water over the cabbage
and cook for 10 minutes. Drain well.
Carefully separate the leaves, so that
you have 12 large leaves.

Cook the tomatoes, chopped
onions and chicken broth cubes over
medium heat in a heavy saucepan
while you prepare the stuffed cabbage.
Mix ground poultry with grated onion,
salt, pepper, rice and the egg. Mix until
well blended. Place a heaping tbs of the
mixture on each cabbage leaf, fold over
the sides and carefully roll up. Place
seam side down in the tomato mixture,
cover and cook over low heat for an
hour. Add the lemon juice and sugar,
cook uncovered for another 30 minutes. Serves 4.

Approximate nutritional analysis per serving:
Calories 647, Protein 39 g,
Carbohydrates 83 g, Fat 19 g,
Cholesterol 132 mg, Sodium 448 mg

Stuffed Cabbage

Cajun Turkey Burgers

CAJUN TURKEY BURGERS

vegetable cooking spray
2 lbs (910 g) NORBEST
    Ground Turkey
2 tbs (30 ml) Worcestershire
    sauce
4 tsp (60 ml) Creole seasoning,
    divided
1 - 14½ oz can (435 g) stewed
    tomatoes, drained
1 tsp (5 ml) minced garlic
8 hamburger buns, toasted

Spray cold grill rack with vegetable
cooking spray. Preheat charcoal grill
for direct-heat cooking.

In medium bowl combine turkey,
Worcestershire sauce and 2 tsp Creole
seasoning. Evenly divide turkey mixture
into 8 burgers, approximately 3½
inches in diameter. Grill turkey burgers
5-6 minutes per side or until 160°F
(71°C) is reached on meat thermometer
and meat is no longer pink in center.

In small saucepan, over medium-
high heat, combine tomatoes, remaining Creole seasoning and garlic. Cook
5 minutes or until most of liquid is
evaporated. To serve, place burger on
bottom half of each bun, drizzle 3 tbs
sauce over burger and top with other
half of buns. Serves 8.

Approximate nutritional analysis per serving:
Calories 337, Protein 25 g,
Carbohydrates 27 g, Fat 14 g,
Cholesterol 57 mg, Sodium 782 mg

BURRITO TURKEY BURGERS

vegetable cooking spray
2 lbs (910 g) NORBEST
    Ground Turkey
1 - 4 oz can (120 g) chopped
    green chilies, drained
1 cup (240 ml) chopped onions
1 - 1¼ oz pkg (47 g) taco
    seasoning mix
8 medium flour tortillas
1 - 16 oz can (480 g) no-fat
    refried beans
shredded lettuce
½ cup (120 ml) grated no-fat
    cheddar cheese
salsa, optional

Spray cold grill rack with vegetable cooking spray. Preheat charcoal grill for direct-heat cooking.

In medium bowl combine turkey, chilies, onion and seasoning mix. Evenly divide turkey mixture into 8 - 9x2-inch rectangular-shaped burgers. Grill burgers 3-4 minutes, turn and continue cooking 2-3 minutes or until 160°F (71°C) is reached on meat thermometer and meat is no longer pink in center. Remove and keep warm. Heat tortillas according to pkg directions. Spread each tortilla with ¼ cup refried beans and sprinkle with lettuce. Place burgers in center of each tortilla and sprinkle 1 tbs of cheese over top. Fold sides of tortilla over burger to create a burrito. Serve with salsa. Serves 8.

Approximate nutritional analysis per serving: Calories 387, Protein 29 g, Carbohydrates 33 g, Fat 14 g, Cholesterol 58 mg, Sodium 946 mg

Burrito Turkey Burgers

QUICK TURKEY CURRY WITH RICE

3 tbs (45 ml) butter
¼ cup (60 ml) minced onion
2-3 tsp (10-15 ml) curry powder
¼ tsp (1 ml) ground ginger
3 tbs (45 ml) flour
½ tsp (3 ml) salt
1 cup (240 ml) milk
1 cup (240 ml) chicken broth
2 cups (480 ml) diced
    cooked turkey
½ tsp (3 ml) lemon juice
1 cup (240 ml) Natural or
    Golden Raisins
4 cups (960 ml) cooked rice

CONDIMENTS, CHOICE OF:
crumbled crisp bacon
shredded hard-cooked eggs
chopped green onion
chopped nuts
coconut
chopped raw vegetables

In 2-qt bowl, place butter, onion, curry powder and ginger; microwave on HIGH 2 minutes. Stir in flour and salt; microwave 90 seconds longer on HIGH, stirring after 45 seconds. Gradually stir in broth and milk. Microwave on HIGH 6-8 minutes, stirring every minute until thick and bubbly. Stir in turkey, lemon juice and raisins; microwave on HIGH for 1 minute longer. Serve over rice, or serve rice and curry in separate bowls. Offer condiments for each person to add on top. Serves 4.

Approximate nutritional analysis per serving: Calories 514, Protein 10 g, Carbohydrates 94 g, Fat 12 g, Cholesterol 32 mg, Sodium 532 mg

Courtesy of The California Raisin Advisory Board.

STUFFED CABBAGE ROLLS WITH YOGURT-DILL SAUCE

1 - 3 lb (1.4 kg) head green
    cabbage, cored
2 tbs (30 ml) olive oil
3 large green onions, sliced
2 large garlic cloves, minced
1 lb (455 g) ground lamb
2 cups (480 ml) plain yogurt
4 tbs (60 ml) fresh snipped dill
1 ½ tsp (8 ml) TABASCO pepper
    sauce
1 ½ tsp (8 ml) salt

Over high heat, heat a large pot of water to boiling. Add cabbage, core-end down. Reduce heat to medium. Cover and simmer until leaves are softened, 10-12 minutes. Remove cabbage to bowl of cold water. Separate 16 large leaves from the head of the cabbage. Trim the tough ribs on the back of leaves so that they will roll up easily. Chop enough of the remaining cabbage to make 3 cups.

In 12-inch skillet over medium heat, in hot oil, cook chopped cabbage, green onions and garlic until tender, about 10 minutes, stirring occasionally. With slotted spoon, remove to bowl. In drippings remaining in skillet over high heat, cook ground lamb until well browned on all sides, stirring frequently. Remove to bowl with cabbage.

In food processor, blend lamb mixture until finely ground. In large bowl toss lamb mixture with ½ cup yogurt, 2 tbs dill, TABASCO pepper sauce, and salt to mix well. Place 3 tbs lamb mixture at bottom of cabbage leaf and roll up tightly to form a 3-inch-long roll, tucking ends in as you roll. Repeat with remaining lamb and leaves.

Preheat oven to 400°F (205°C). Place cabbage rolls on rack in a roasting pan. Add 1 cup boiling water; cover pan tightly with foil. Bake 20 minutes or until rolls are hot. Meanwhile, in medium bowl combine remaining 1 ½ cups yogurt and 2 tbs dill. To serve, remove cabbage rolls to platter; top with Yogurt-Dill Sauce. Serves 4.

Approximate nutritional analysis per serving: Calories 309, Protein 28 g, Carbohydrates 18 g, Fat 14 g, Cholesterol 66 mg, Sodium 971 mg

SPICED MEATBALLS AND MAPLE-Y BEANS

MEATBALLS:
½ lb (230 g) lean ground beef
½ lb (230 g) Italian sausage,
    skinned
1 cup (240 ml) fine bread crumbs
½ cup (120 ml) milk
2 tbs (30 ml) onion, chopped
2 eggs, lightly beaten
1 tsp (5 ml) salt
½ tsp (3 ml) nutmeg
¼ tsp (1 ml) black pepper
¼ tsp (1 ml) allspice
3 tbs (45 ml) GOYA Vegetable Oil
    for frying

2 cans GOYA Pinto Beans,
    drained
¼ cup (60 ml) GOYA Cider
    Vinegar
¼ cup (60 ml) maple syrup

Combine all ingredients for meatballs; mix thoroughly. Shape into 16 - 1-inch balls. Heat oil in large frying pan; brown meatballs and remove. Combine beans, vinegar and maple syrup in frying pan. Arrange meatballs on top of beans; bring to boil. Cover and simmer 30 minutes. Serves 4.

Approximate nutritional analysis per serving: Calories 834, Protein 46 g, Carbohydrates 75 g, Fat 39 g, Cholesterol 208 mg, Sodium 241 mg

Opposite: Stuffed Cabbage Rolls with Yogurt-Dill Sauce

GREEK-STYLE LAMB AND BEAN SKILLET DINNER

1 lb (455 g) ground lamb
1 tsp (5 ml) garlic salt
1 tsp (5 ml) Italian seasoning, crushed
1 - 15 oz can (450 g) great northern beans, drained
2 medium tomatoes, chopped
1 cup (240 ml) dry white wine
1 tbs (15 ml) chopped fresh parsley
1 tsp (5 ml) grated lemon peel

Combine ground lamb, garlic salt and Italian seasoning; mix lightly but thoroughly. Pinch off 1½-inch pieces of lamb mixture to make approximately 16 free-form meatballs. Brown meatballs in large non-stick skillet over medium heat. Pour off drippings. Add beans, tomatoes and wine; cook, uncovered, over medium heat 15 minutes, stirring occasionally. Garnish with parsley and lemon peel. Serves 4.

Microwave directions: Reduce wine to ½ cup (120 ml) . Use ½ tsp garlic salt in lamb mixture; reserve remaining ½ tsp garlic salt for bean mixture. Place free-form meatballs around sides of 11¾x7½-inch micro-wave-safe baking dish. Cover with waxed paper and microwave at HIGH 4-5 minutes, rotating dish ¼ turn after 3 minutes.

Remove meatballs with slotted spoon; keep warm. Pour off drippings. Combine beans, tomatoes, wine and reserved ½ tsp garlic salt in same baking dish. Microwave, uncovered, at HIGH 5 minutes, stirring once. Return meatballs to baking dish; continue to microwave at MEDIUM 2 minutes. Garnish with parsley and lemon peel. Serves 4.

Approximate nutritional analysis per serving:
Calories 321, Protein 33 g,
Carbohydrates 20 g, Fat 11 g,
Cholesterol 91 mg, Sodium 879 mg

Courtesy of the National Live Stock and Meat Board.

ZESTY HAMBURGERS

1 lb (455 g) ground beef (or ground turkey)
1½ tsp (8 ml) OLD BAY Seasoning

In a medium bowl, mix together ground beef and OLD BAY Seasoning. Shape into patties. Fry or broil as usual. Serves 6.

Approximate nutritional analysis per serving:
Calories 216, Protein 17 g,
Carbohydrates 0 g, Fat 16 g,
Cholesterol 66 mg, Sodium 134 mg

Greek-Style Lamb and Bean Skillet Dinner

CHILI BLANCO

½ lb (230 g) diced turkey breast
    or ground turkey, optional
1 tbs (15 ml) vegetable oil
½ cup (120 ml) diced celery
½ cup (120 ml) fresh or canned
    Anaheim chilies
½ cup (120 ml) chopped onion
2 cups (480 ml) water
1 - 16 oz can (480 g) white small
    or
    white kidney beans, drained
1 cup (240 ml) seeded and diced
    fresh tomatoes
1 cup (240 ml) seeded and diced
    fresh zucchini
½ tsp (3 ml) salt
½ tsp (3 ml) ground cumin
⅛ tsp (.5 ml) black pepper
⅛ tsp (.5 ml) cayenne pepper
corn or flour tortillas

CONDIMENTS:
shredded lowfat cheese
chopped onion
chopped cilantro
diced tomatoes

Brown ground turkey in oil in medium saucepan; drain excess drippings. Add celery, chilies and onion and cook until tender. Add remaining ingredients except tortillas and condiments; mix well. Bring mixture to boil, reduce heat and simmer 30 minutes or until flavors are blended. Serve with tortillas and condiments. Serves 4.

Approximate nutritional analysis per serving:
Calories 288, Protein 25 g,
Carbohydrates 38 g, Fat 5 g,
Cholesterol 36 mg, Sodium 317 mg

Courtesy California Table Grape Commission

MEATLOAF RING WITH FRENCH ONION SAUCE

1½ lbs (685 g) ground beef *or* 1 lb
    (455 g) ground beef *plus*
    ½ lb (230 g) ground pork
1 small onion, chopped
1 cup (240 ml) fine dry bread
    crumbs
2 eggs, beaten
⅔ cup (160 ml) milk
1 tsp (5 ml) seasoned salt
freshly ground pepper

SAUCE:
2 large onions, thinly sliced
1 tbs (15 ml) butter
1 tsp (5 ml) dried tarragon
½ cup (120 ml) ketchup
¼ cup (60 ml) cider vinegar
reserved meatloaf juices
    (skim off fat)
½ cup (120 ml) Natural raisins

Lightly mix first 7 ingredients and fill a 9-inch microwaveable ring mold, or make a ring by placing a custard cup in the center of a 9-inch baking dish. Cover meat with waxed paper; microwave on MEDIUM-HIGH for 12-14 minutes, rotating dish a quarter turn after 7 minutes and again after 11 minutes. Pour off liquid and fat and save; let meatloaf stand 5-10 minutes while making sauce. Standing allows meat to set-up for easier slicing. Serves 6.

    Sauce: Place onions, butter and tarragon in 1-qt bowl; cover and microwave on HIGH for 5-6 minutes stirring once or twice. Stir in ketchup, vinegar, meat juices and raisins. Cook, uncovered, on HIGH for 2 minutes, until bubbling throughout. Pour on top of entire meatloaf, guiding most of the sauce that drips down into the open center of the ring.

Approximate nutritional analysis per serving:
Calories 531, Protein 35 g,
Carbohydrates 39 g, Fat 27 g,
Cholesterol 179 mg, Sodium 847 mg

Courtesy of the California Raisin Advisory Board.

Chili Blanco

Hamburger Update

HAMBURGER UPDATE

**¼ cup plus 1 tbs (75 ml)
     DANNON plain nonfat yogurt
1 oz (30 g) crumbled feta cheese
½ tsp (3 ml) ground cumin
1 lb (455 g) extra lean
     ground beef
¼ cup (60 ml) minced green
     onion
¼ cup (60 ml) cilantro leaves,
     minced
1 large clove garlic, minced
1 tbs (15 ml) grated fresh
     ginger root
4 lettuce leaves
20 very thin slices peeled
     cucumber
2 onion rolls, split and toasted**

Combine yogurt, cheese and cumin;
blend with a fork until cheese is finely
crumbled. Cover and chill at least
1 hour. Combine low fat ground beef
and next 4 ingredients, mixing well.
Shape into 4 - ½-inch-thick patties.
Cook in non-stick skillet or grill 3
inches from heat 6-7 minutes on each
side or until meat and juices are no
longer pink. Place a lettuce leaf, 5 slices
of cucumber, and beef patty on each
bun half. Top each patty with 2 tbs
yogurt mixture. Serve immediately.
Serves 4.

*Approximate nutritional analysis per serving:
Calories 232, Protein 27 g,
Carbohydrates 21 g, Fat 7 g,
Cholesterol 62 mg, Sodium 458 mg*

BRONZED HAMBURGERS

**4 tbs (60 ml) unsalted butter
or margarine
2 small yellow onions, coarsely
chopped
2 lbs (910 g) ground round,
ground chuck, ground veal,
or very lean ground beef,
at room temperature
2 tbs (30 ml) CHEF PAUL
PRUDHOMME'S Meat Magic
6 hamburger buns or onion rolls
shredded lettuce
sliced tomatoes
sliced red onions
mayonnaise
Creole mustard, or Dijon or
yellow mustard**

Melt the butter in a small sauté pan over medium heat. Add the coarsely chopped onion and sauté until transparent. Reduce the heat and continue to cook until the onions are golden brown, about 15 minutes. You should end up with about ¾ cup caramelized onions. Set aside.

Place the ground meat in a large mixing bowl. Sprinkle 1 tbs of the Meat Magic over the meat and work it in well. Sprinkle the remaining 1 tbs Meat Magic into the meat and mix well until thoroughly incorporated. Add the onions to the meat mixture and combine. Form the meat into 6 patties about 6 oz each and about ¾-inch thick.

Heat a heavy griddle or large, heavy aluminum or electric skillet to 350°F (180°C). Hamburgers will not stick to the surface if griddle is very hot. Place about 4 patties on the griddle or skillet surface and cook for 3 minutes. Turn and cook another 3 minutes for medium rare. For medium, cook 4 minutes per side. Place the patties on a serving platter, then wipe the griddle or skillet surface thoroughly before cooking the remaining patties. Serve immediately with all the traditional trimmings. Serves 6.

* About Bronzing: Bronzing is a good technique that works wonderfully for meat and fish - and it's so simple. In order to lock in juices, you actually brown very quickly one side of the meat or fish at a time on a heavy griddle or in a large, heavy aluminum skillet or electric fry-pan heated to 350°F (180°C). If you omit the butter stages, bronzing is an exceptional way to cook delicious reduced fat diet food. Just coat the meat or seafood with a non-stick vegetable spray and season as recipe indicates.

*Approximate nutritional analysis per serving:
Calories 391, Protein 36 g,
Carbohydrates 21 g, Fat 17 g,
Cholesterol 114 mg, Sodium 342 mg*

Bronzed Hamburgers

SWEET AND SOUR CRANBERRY MEATBALLS

1½ lbs (685 g) lean ground meat
    (beef, pork, mutton, or a
    mixture of any)
⅔ cup (160 ml) fine dry
    bread crumbs
½ cup (120 ml) milk
2 medium eggs
½ tsp (3 ml) garlic powder
½ tsp (3 ml) pepper
1 tsp (5 ml) salt

SWEET AND SOUR SAUCE:
1 - 16 oz can (480 g) whole berry
    cranberry sauce
1 - 8 oz can (240 g) crushed
    pineapple
1 - 12 oz bottle (360 ml) chili
    sauce

Mix first 7 ingredients together,
blending thoroughly, and set aside to
"ripen" while mixing Sweet and Sour
Sauce. Mix fruit and chili sauce well;
heat slowly in large shallow pan so that
meatballs are not piled too deeply.
Shape meat mixture into 1-inch balls.
DO NOT BROWN; place gently in
heated sauce and simmer until well
cooked and sauce is thickened. During
early stages of cooking, stir meatballs
very gently so they will hold their
shape. Yields 70 meatballs, serves 6.

Approximate nutritional analysis per serving:
Calories 576, Protein 33 g,
Carbohydrates 57 g, Fat 24 g,
Cholesterol 173 mg, Sodium 1038 mg

Courtesy of the Cape Cod Cranberry
Growers' Association.

**Sweet and Sour
Cranberry Meatballs**

Saucy Meatballs

SAUCY MEATBALLS

1 lb (455 g) lean ground beef
⅔ cup (160 ml) grated Parmesan
    cheese
½ cup (120 ml) seasoned dry
    bread crumbs
½ cup (120 ml) milk
1 egg, slightly beaten
1 tbs (15 ml) vegetable oil
2 - 14½ oz cans (840 g) stewed
    tomatoes,
    cut into bite-size pieces
⅓ cup (80 ml) HEINZ 57 Sauce
½ tsp (3 ml) salt
⅛ tsp (.5 ml) pepper
hot buttered noodles

Combine first 5 ingredients. Form into
20 meatballs using a rounded tbs for
each. Brown in oil; drain excess fat.
Combine tomatoes, 57 Sauce, salt and
pepper; pour over meatballs. Simmer,
uncovered, 15-20 minutes or until
sauce is desired consistency, stirring
occasionally. Serve meatballs and sauce
over noodles. Serves 5.

Approximate nutritional analysis per serving
w/o noodles: Calories 382, Protein 28 g,
Carbohydrates 17 g, Fat 23 g,
Cholesterol 126 mg, Sodium 709 mg

MEATBALLS WITH CRANBERRY-APRICOT SAUCE

1 lb (455 g) ground turkey
½ cup (120 ml) dry bread crumbs
⅓ cup (80 ml) onion, finely chopped
¼ cup (60 ml) milk
1 egg
2 tbs (30 ml) dried parsley flakes
1 tsp (5 ml) poultry seasoning
1 tsp (5 ml) Worcestershire sauce
dash salt and pepper

SAUCE:
1 cup (240 ml) ketchup
1 - 12 oz jar (360 g) apricot preserves
½ cup (120 ml) Dried Cranberries

Mix together ground turkey, bread crumbs, onion, milk, egg, parsley flakes, poultry seasoning, Worcestershire sauce, salt and pepper. Shape into 1-inch balls. Brown meatballs in a large non-stick skillet over medium heat until done. Remove meatballs from pan. Remove any fat from pan. Heat ketchup and apricot preserves in skillet, stirring until blended. Add Dried Cranberries to the sauce mixture. Add meatballs and stir until coated with sauce. Simmer uncovered 30 minutes, stirring occasionally. Yields 30-40 meatballs.

Approximate nutritional analysis per meatball:
Calories 67, Protein 4 g,
Carbohydrates 8 g, Fat 2 g,
Cholesterol 15 mg, Sodium 108 mg

SCANDINAVIAN MEATBALLS

1½ cups (355 ml) DANNON Plain Nonfat or Lowfat Yogurt
½ cup (120 ml) soft bread crumbs
1 lb (455 g) lean ground beef
1 egg
¼ cup (60 ml) finely chopped onion
¼ tsp (1 ml) salt, optional
2 tbs (30 ml) all-purpose flour
1 - 3½ g envelope instant beef broth mix
1 tsp (5 ml) Worcestershire sauce
snipped fresh parsley, optional

In a large bowl combine ½ cup yogurt and bread crumbs; let stand 5 minutes. Add ground beef, egg, onion and salt.

Mix well and shape into 1¼-inch meatballs. Spray a large nonstick skillet with vegetable cooking spray. Cook meatballs over medium heat until brown and cooked through, turning often; drain. Wipe skillet dry.

In a small bowl, combine 1 cup yogurt, flour, beef broth mix and Worcestershire sauce until smooth. Add to skillet. Cook over medium-low heat, stirring constantly, until thickened. Do not boil. Reduce heat to low. Add meatballs; mix with sauce and cook until just heated through. If desired, garnish with parsley. Serves 6.

Approximate nutritional analysis per serving:
Calories 301, Protein 24 g,
Carbohydrates 13 g, Fat 16 g,
Cholesterol 105 mg, Sodium 429 mg

Scandinavian Meatballs

SOUTHWEST MEATLOAF

1 lb (455 g) lean ground beef
½ lb (230 g) chorizo or
    Italian sausage
½ cup (120 ml) quick-cooking or
    regular rolled oats
½ cup (120 ml) chopped onion
2 eggs, beaten
1 - 16 oz jar (480 ml) CHI-CHI'S
    Salsa, divided
1½ cups (355 ml) CHI-CHI'S
    Refried Beans
1 cup (240 ml) shredded cheddar
    cheese
2 tbs (30 ml) CHI-CHI'S Diced
    Green Chilies

Heat oven to 350°F (180°C). Line 9x5-inch loaf pan with enough foil so that it extends beyond the pan edges. Coat foil with nonstick cooking spray. In medium bowl, combine ground beef, sausage, oats, onion, eggs and 2 tbs salsa. Press half of the mixture into prepared pan. Form a 1-inch deep indentation down center of meat mixture, leaving a 1-inch border of meat on all sides. In a small bowl, combine refried beans, cheese and chilies. Mix well. Spoon bean mixture into indentation, mounding mixture if necessary. Press remaining meat mixture evenly over beans and meat, sealing edges. Bake 1¼ hours or until well done. Let stand 15 minutes. Lift loaf from pan using foil. Remove foil. Spoon remaining salsa on top of meatloaf. Serves 6.

Approximate nutritional analysis per serving:
Calories 530, Protein 33 g,
Carbohydrates 19 g, Fat 35 g,
Cholesterol 170 mg, Sodium 1230 mg

Southwest Meatloaf

STUFFED CABBAGE WITH OLIVES

1 - 2 lb (910 g) head cabbage
½ cup (120 ml) water
1 lb (455 g) lean ground pork
   or beef
¼ cup (60 ml) packaged dry
   bread crumbs
1 tsp (5 ml) oregano
1 cup (240 ml) sliced
   CALIFORNIA ripe olives
1⅔ cups (400 ml) spaghetti sauce

Place cabbage in microwave-safe dish or bowl large enough to hold it. Add water, cover with plastic wrap and cook at HIGH for 6-8 minutes, turning once halfway through, or until outer leaves flex easily. Drain and run under cold water to cool enough to handle. Gently remove 8 large outer leaves. Chop enough of remaining cabbage to get about 1 cup. Save any leftover for other uses. Combine chopped cabbage with pork, bread crumbs, oregano and half the olives and sauce. Roll leaves around filling to make closed packages. Cover with plastic wrap and heat at HIGH for 14-16 minutes, or until hot, rearranging rolls halfway through. Heat remaining sauce in large measuring cup, covered with paper towel to prevent splattering, for 1½-2 minutes. Transfer rolls to platter or plates, ribbon sauce over and sprinkle with remaining olives.
Serves 4.

Approximate nutritional analysis per serving:
Calories 401, Protein 41 g,
Carbohydrates 22 g, Fat 17 g,
Cholesterol 130 mg, Sodium 401 mg

FIESTA MEAT LOAF

1 lb (455 g) extra lean
   ground beef
¾ cup (180 ml) quick oats
½ cup (120 ml) HEALTHY
   CHOICE Cholesterol Free
   Egg Product
¼ cup (60 ml) salsa
½ cup (120 ml) diced green
   pepper
¼ cup (60 ml) diced onion
1 tbs (15 ml) chili powder
½ tsp (3 ml) salt
¼ cup (60 ml) salsa

In medium bowl, combine beef, oats, egg product, ¼ cup salsa, green pepper, onion, chili powder and salt. Form meat mixture into loaf shape and place in a 8x4x3-inch loaf dish sprayed with vegetable oil spray. Top with ¼ cup salsa. Bake in 350°F (180°C) oven for 55 minutes. Serves 6.

Approximate nutritional analysis per serving:
Calories 150, Protein 18 g,
Carbohydrates 8 g, Fat 4 g,
Cholesterol 35 mg, Sodium 400 mg

Fiesta Meatloaf

PIMIENTOS RELLENOS
Stuffed Peppers

1 small onion, minced
¼ cup (60 ml) GOYA Olive Oil
1 clove garlic, minced
¼ lb (115 g) ground beef
¼ lb (115 g) ground veal
1 GOYA Chorizo, chopped
2 tbs (30 ml) GOYA Sofrito
1 packet Sazón GOYA sin Achiote
1 tbs (15 ml) pine nuts
2 tbs (30 ml) GOYA Tomato
Sauce
¼ cup (60 ml) GOYA Medium
Rice, cooked
salt and pepper to taste
6 whole medium bell peppers,
tops cut off,
seeds and veins removed

In skillet, sauté onion slowly in 2 tbs olive oil until translucent. Add garlic, ground beef, veal, chorizo, Sofrito, Sazón, pine nuts and tomato sauce. Cook 5-10 minutes over medium heat, until meat is done. Stir in cooked rice; add salt and pepper to taste. Spoon meat mixture into peppers. Place into a shallow greased pan and bake at 350°F (180°C) for 5-10 minutes. Serve drizzled with olive oil if desired. Serves 6.

Approximate nutritional analysis per serving:
Calories 512, Protein 26 g,
Carbohydrates 12 g, Fat 40 g,
Cholesterol 96 mg, Sodium 1366 mg

Pimientos Rellenos

MIKI'S CHILI

2 cans GOYA Red Kidney Beans,
    drained
1½ lbs (685 g) ground beef
3 tbs (45 ml) GOYA Vegetable Oil
2 large onions, chopped
2 green peppers, chopped
2 red peppers, chopped
3 cloves garlic, whole
1 - 2 lb can (910 g) whole
    tomatoes, cut up
dash cayenne pepper
2 tbs (30 ml) chili powder
2 tbs (30 ml) chili seasoning
1 tsp (5 ml) sugar

Heat oil in large skillet, brown meat.
Add onions, red and green pepper,
garlic, tomatoes and seasonings. Bring
to boil, and simmer at least 2 hours.
Add beans before last half hour.
Serves 6.

Approximate nutritional analysis per serving:
Calories 593, Protein 40 g,
Carbohydrates 45 g, Fat 29 g,
Cholesterol 99 mg, Sodium 919 mg

CHILI WITH BLACK BEANS

2 cans GOYA Black Beans,
    not drained
3 lbs (1.4 kg) chuck steak cut in
    ½-inch cubes
¼ cup (60 ml) GOYA Extra Virgin
    Olive Oil
2 onions, chopped
1 canned jalapeño, seeded and
    minced
1 - 8 oz can (240 ml) GOYA
    Tomato Sauce
3 tbs (45 ml) chili powder
¼ cup (60 ml) red wine
1 tsp (5 ml) dry mustard
2 cloves garlic, minced
½ tsp (3 ml) ground cumin
black pepper to taste

In large heavy casserole, heat oil and
sauté onions and pepper. Add beef and
brown lightly. Add remaining ingredients except beans and simmer 30-45
minutes. Add beans, cover and simmer
30 minutes. Serves 8.

Approximate nutritional analysis per serving:
Calories 695, Protein 47 g,
Carbohydrates 9 g, Fat 51 g,
Cholesterol 168 mg, Sodium 204 mg

Miki's Chili

SMOKY CHILI

1 cup (240 ml) sliced celery
1 tbs (15 ml) vegetable oil
½ lb (230 g) Polish smoked
    sausage, quartered length
    wise, cut into ¼-inch slices
1 large green bell pepper,
    coarsely chopped
1 large onion, chopped
1 tbs (15 ml) chili powder
1 - 14½ oz can (435 g) tomatoes,
    cut into bite-size pieces
1 - 15 oz can (450 g) spicy chili
    beans
½ cup (120 ml) HEINZ Chili
    Sauce
hot cooked rice

In 4-qt Dutch oven, sauté celery in oil 5
minutes. Add sausage, bell pepper and
onion; sauté until vegetables are tender,
about 4 minutes stirring occasionally.
Stir in chili powder, tomatoes, beans
and chili sauce; simmer, uncovered,
15 minutes, stirring occasionally. Serve
over rice. Serves 4.

Approximate nutritional analysis per serving:
Calories 395, Protein 17 g,
Carbohydrates 40 g, Fat 20 g,
Cholesterol 38 mg, Sodium 1724 mg

Smoky Chili

FIERY POT TEXAS CHILI

2 lbs (910 g) chili meat*
**¼ cup (60 ml) cooking oil,
    divided**
1½ cups (355 ml) water or beer
1 - 8 oz can (240 ml) tomato sauce
2 small onions, chopped
**1 medium green pepper,
    finely chopped**
5-6 cloves garlic, minced
1 tsp (5 ml) oregano
**1 tbs (15 ml) ground cumin,
    or to taste**
4 tbs (60 ml) chili powder
1 tsp (5 ml) salt
**½ tsp (3 ml) IMPERIAL
    Granulated Sugar**
red pepper (cayenne) to taste
**4-5 medium jalapeño peppers,
    chopped**

* Chili meat is coarsely ground round
steak or well-trimmed chuck steak.

In large skillet, brown meat in one half
of the oil. Transfer the meat to a large
kettle or electric slow-cooker, leaving
liquid in skillet. Add water or beer and
tomato sauce to meat; sauté onion,
green pepper, garlic in remaining oil
and liquid in skillet. Add remaining dry
ingredients and chopped jalapeño
peppers. Simmer about 30 minutes,
then transfer to kettle. Simmer about
2 hours. Dip off grease that rises to top.
Serves 8.

Note: Red pepper and jalapeño
peppers are the "zingers" in this recipe.
Add both with caution.

Approximate nutritional analysis per serving:
Calories 409, Protein 30 g,
Carbohydrates 8 g, Fat 28 g,
Cholesterol 95 mg, Sodium 804 mg

Fiery Pot Texas Chili

CHILI AND THEN SOME

**2 cans GOYA Red Kidney Beans,
    drained**
1 lb (455 g) ground beef
**1 lb (455 g) Italian hot sausage,
    skinned**
**2 tbs (30 ml) GOYA Extra Virgin
    Olive Oil**
2 cups (480 ml) onion, chopped
**1 cup (240 ml) green pepper,
    chopped**
1 cup (240 ml) celery, chopped
2 cloves garlic, minced
3 tbs (45 ml) chili powder
1 tbs (15 ml) oregano
2 bay leaves
2 tsp (10 ml) ground cumin
**3 cups (720 ml) canned tomatoes
    in purée**
1 cup (240 ml) beef broth
salt and pepper to taste

Heat oil in heavy skillet; add meat and
brown. Add remaining ingredients
except beans, and blend well. Bring to
boil and simmer 20 minutes, stirring
frequently. Add beans and simmer 15
minutes longer. Serves 8.

Approximate nutritional analysis per serving:
Calories 552, Protein 33 g,
Carbohydrates 30 g, Fat 34 g,
Cholesterol 97 mg, Sodium 1503 mg

EMPAÑADAS GRANDE

1 tbs (15 ml) olive oil
1 lb (455 g) ground turkey
½ cup (120 ml) chopped onion
2 cloves garlic, minced
**1 cup (240 ml) CHI-CHI'S
    Pico de Gallo**
**½ cup (120 ml) cooked
    garbanzo beans**
**½ cup (120 ml) chopped
    tart apple**
¼ cup (60 ml) golden raisins
2 tbs (30 ml) slivered almonds
2 tbs (30 ml) chopped fresh mint
2 tbs (30 ml) chopped fresh basil
1 - 16 oz pkg (480 g) hot roll mix
1¼ cups (294 ml) water
2 tbs (30 ml) vegetable oil
**1¾ cups (415 ml) shredded sharp
    cheddar cheese**
CHI-CHI'S Salsa, if desired
sour cream, if desired

In large skillet, heat oil over medium-
high heat. Cook turkey, onion and
garlic until turkey is no longer pink;
drain. Stir in Pico de Gallo, beans,
apple, raisins, almonds, mint and basil.
Cook and stir over low heat until
heated through. Stir in 1 cup shredded
cheese. Set aside.

Prepare hot roll mix according to
package directions except eliminate the
egg and 1¼ cups (295 ml) water and 2
tbs (30 ml) oil. After mixing dough and
kneading 4 times, gradually knead in ¾
cup of shredded cheese. Cover dough
with bowl; let rise 5 minutes. Heat oven
to 425°F (220°C). Grease 2 large
baking sheets.

Divide dough in half. Roll each
piece into 10-inch circle. Place dough
circles on baking sheets. Spoon half of
turkey mixture and half of the remaining cheese onto half of one circle.
Repeat with remaining dough circle,
turkey mixture and cheese. Brush edge
of dough circles with water. Fold dough
in half; seal edges with finger, fork or
pastry crimper.

Bake one empañada at a time on
lower oven rack 12-18 minutes or until
golden brown. Keep second empañada
in refrigerator; covered with plastic
wrap, until ready to bake. Cut into
wedges to serve. Serve with salsa and
sour cream, if desired. Serves 6.

Approximate nutritional analysis per serving:
Calories 640, Protein 32 g,
Carbohydrates 70 g, Fat 26 g,
Cholesterol 80 mg, Sodium 660 mg

Opposite: Empañadas Grande

MESQUITE CHICKEN BURGERS

1 lb (455 g) PREMIUM YOUNG 'N TENDER Brand Boneless, Skinless Chicken Thighs, ground
½ lb (120 g) bulk pork sausage, spicy or hot
1¼ tsp (6 ml) mesquite seasoning salt, or to taste

APRICOT-PEPPER CHUTNEY:
¾ cup (180 ml) apricot preserves
2 tbs (30 ml) balsamic vinegar
1 tbs (15 ml) Dijon mustard
1 tsp (5 ml) grated fresh ginger
_or_ ¼ tsp (1 ml) ground ginger
1 tsp (5 ml) minced garlic
1 tsp (5 ml) fresh thyme _or_
¼ tsp (1 ml) dried thyme
¼ cup (60 ml) finely chopped red bell pepper
¼ cup (60 ml) finely chopped sweet onions
2 tsp (10 ml) finely chopped jalapeño peppers
4 Kaiser or onion rolls, split
Dijon mustard

Combine chicken, sausage and mesquite salt. Shape into four patties, chill at least 20 minutes.

Chutney: combine preserves, vinegar, mustard, ginger and garlic in a small saucepan. Heat to simmering and cook about 3 minutes. Remove from heat and add thyme, red pepper, onion and jalapeño pepper. Set aside.

Grill chicken burgers over medium coals until juices run clear, turning as needed. Lightly toast rolls on grill and spread with mustard. Serve chicken burgers with chutney. Serves 4.

Note: You may have butcher grind thighs for you or use food processor with metal blade attachment. Burgers may be cooked in oven broiler or on stove top if preferred.

Approximate nutritional analysis per serving:
Calories 760, Protein 55 g,
Carbohydrates 78 g, Fat 25 g,
Cholesterol 138 mg, Sodium 171 mg

MICROWAVE TURKEY MEAT BALLS

1 lb (455 g) EMPIRE KOSHER Ground Turkey
¼ tsp (1 ml) minced garlic
½ tsp (3 ml) minced onion
2 tbs (30 ml) dry kosher parve bread crumbs
2 tbs (30 ml) parve spaghetti sauce
salt and pepper, if desired

Mix all ingredients together, shape into meat balls a little larger than a golf ball. Cook in microwave on HIGH for 3 minutes. Spoon additional spaghetti sauce over top, cook another 4 minutes on HIGH. Season with salt and pepper if desired.

Approximate nutritional analysis per serving:
Calories 276, Protein 28 g,
Carbohydrates 3 g, Fat 16 g,
Cholesterol 78 mg, Sodium 119 mg

MEDITERRANEAN TURKEY AND EGGPLANT STIR-FRY

1 lb (455 g) EMPIRE KOSHER Ground Turkey or Ground Chicken
1 cup (240 ml) onion thinly sliced
2 cloves garlic, minced
1½ tsp (8 ml) oregano _or_ 3 tsp (15 ml) fresh oregano
1 tsp fresh mint, chopped
pepper and salt to taste
4 cups (960 ml) eggplant or zucchini, in cubes
1 cup (240 ml) green pepper, cut into ½-inch strips
1 tbs (165 ml) olive oil
1 tsp (5 ml) sugar
1 medium ripe tomato, peeled, in wedges

In large skillet, sauté ground turkey or chicken over medium-high heat with onion, garlic, oregano, mint and pepper 5-6 minutes or until meat is no longer pink. Remove turkey mixture from skillet and set aside. In the same skillet, over medium-high heat, sauté eggplant and green pepper in oil 4 minutes or until vegetables are crisp-tender. Combine turkey mixture with vegetable mixture and add tomato and sugar. Cook over medium-high heat, about 5 minutes, or until heated through. Serves 4.

Approximate nutritional analysis per serving:
Calories 348, Protein 30 g,
Carbohydrates 14 g, Fat 19 g,
Cholesterol 78 mg, Sodium 103 mg